LET'S GO TEAM:
Cheer, Dance, March

LET'S GO TEAM:
Cheer, Dance, March

CHANTS, CHEERS, and JUMPS

Craig Peters

Mason Crest Publishers
Philadelphia

To Alexandra: We're cheering for you all the time, whether you realize it or not.

Mason Crest Publishers, Inc.
370 Reed Road
Broomall, PA 19008
(866) MCP-BOOK (toll free)
www.masoncrest.com

3 4 5 6 7 8 9 10

Library of Congress Cataloging-in-Publication Data

Peters, Craig, 1958-
  Chants, cheers, and jumps / Craig Peters.
      v. cm. — (Let's go team—cheer, dance, march)
Includes index.
Contents: Where it all began — Chants — Cheers — Jumps — Making your own chants and cheers.
  ISBN 1-59084-535-8
  1. Cheerleading—Juvenile literature. 2. Cheers—Juvenile literature.
[1. Cheerleading. 2. Cheers.] I. Title. II. Series.
  LB3635 .P433 2003
  791.6'4—dc21

                                            2002015955

Produced by
Choptank Syndicate and Chestnut Productions
226 South Washington Street
Easton, Maryland 21601

Project Editors Norman Macht and Mary Hull
Design Lisa Hochstein
Picture Research Mary Hull

Printed and bound in the Hashemite Kingdom of Jordan

OPPOSITE TITLE PAGE

Stunts, when performed safely and correctly, can complement cheers and add to the visual effect of cheerleading.

Table of Contents

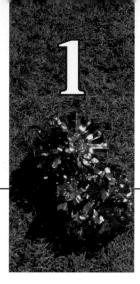

Where It All Began

Cheering for favorites in competitions has probably been going on for thousands of years, since the first men tried to outrace or outthrow one another. Runners in the first Olympic Games in Greece in 776 B.C. had their fans rooting for them. When North American Indian tribes settled disputes by playing hard-fought, exhausting lacrosse games, the women cheered for their warriors (and whipped them with sticks if they tired or faltered during the action).

The first known American college cheer was invented in the 1880s by a pep club at Princeton University. Students at the football game sang out:

Whether they are cheering at sports events or cheerleading competitions, cheerleaders generate enthusiasm and positive energy.

Rah rah rah

Tiger Tiger Tiger

Sis sis sis

Boom boom boom

Aaaahhhhh!

Princeton! Princeton! Princeton!

The cheer was said to have been inspired by a Civil War chant and was performed in what has been described as a "locomotive style."

As the popularity of college football grew, the practice of chanting and cheering catchy phrases by onlookers spread to other schools. But it was spontaneous and disorganized; there were no leaders.

At a game one day in 1898, a first-year University of Minnesota medical student named Jack Campbell was inspired to leap out onto the field during a time out and lead his team's supporters' cheering efforts. Like a choirmaster or band leader, he waved his arms and called out:

Rah Rah Rah

Sku-u-mah Hoo-rah

Hoo-Rah!

Varsity! Varsity!

Minn-e-so-tah!

The few hundred students in the bleachers eagerly followed his lead. They cheered louder and with more enthusiasm than ever. Harnessing the energy that had been scattered, Jack Campbell lifted spirits and helped to motivate his team on to victory. That's the kind of effect that good cheerleading can have on a team.

Cheerleading is more than getting the crowds to yell cheers, though. Cheerleading is about leadership and being a role model. Cheerleaders spark enthusiasm when they cheer and chant, providing positive energy when it's most needed, inspiring a positive outlook when their team is losing a game.

For the cheerleaders themselves, cheerleading is about personal growth and self-confidence, friendship and accomplishment.

"Cheerleading has evolved past the negative stereotype of clueless cute girls bouncing up and down on the sidelines," wrote Linda Rae Chappell in *Coaching Cheerleading Successfully*. "Cheering in the 21st century

CHEERS OR CHANTS: WHAT'S THE DIFFERENCE?

Some people use the terms "cheers" and "chants" to mean the same thing. This is incorrect.

A cheer is longer than a chant, and is performed when the ball is not in play. Cheers often feature stunts. Think of what football cheerleaders might be doing on the sidelines during a time out on the field, and you'll have a pretty good idea of what makes a cheer.

A chant is a short phrase, repeated in response to something that happens on the field. Think of a football team that has just scored a touchdown. The defending team's cheerleaders will probably be chanting, "Block that point! Block that point!"

HISTORICAL HIGHLIGHTS

Here are some notable highlights in the history of cheerleading:

1870s: First pep club formed at Princeton University.

1880s: First known cheer created.

1920s: Gymnastics begins to be incorporated into cheerleading routines. Women start to be included in the formerly all-male activity.

1930s: Paper pom pons are introduced.

1940s: Cheerleading becomes mainly a female activity.

1948: Lawrence R. Herkimer starts the National Cheerleaders Association in his hometown of Dallas, Texas.

1949: Herkimer organizes the first cheerleader camp at Sam Houston State University in Huntsville, Texas.

1950s: The Baltimore Colts football team organizes the first pro cheerleading squad.

1960s: The vinyl pom pon is created.

1976: The Dallas Cowboys Cheerleaders perform at Super Bowl X.

1978: The CBS television network broadcasts the Collegiate Cheerleading Championships, held by the International Cheerleading Foundation. The broadcast draws more attention to cheerleading than ever before.

1980s: The first national cheerleading competitions are established.

2000: The inaugural World Cheerleading Championship is held. The movie *Bring It On* is released.

2002: Competitive cheerleading becomes the fastest-growing girls' sport in the United States, according to the National Federation of State High School Associations; as many as 400,000 cheerleaders attend cheer camps each year.

A chant is a short repetitive phrase used in response to the action in a game. In contrast, cheers are performed only when there is a break in the game.

promises even more excitement because males and females are developing their athletic abilities along with their leadership skills to provide good role models for all of America's youth."

Cheerleading squads are changing. Many split their time between cheering at games and cheering at competitions. Other squads exist only to cheer at competitions. Whether the squads are appearing at games or competitions, though, one thing never changes: cheerleaders generate enthusiasm and excitement.

Chants

Think of chants as mini-cheers. Chants, sometimes called "sidelines," are short and to the point. They are most often performed during a game in response to a specific thing that happens in the action. Usually chants are performed three or more times in a row.

Many times, squads will add hand claps, clasps, or foot stomps to the chant to add rhythm and help the fans get into the chant. A clap is when you slap your hands together with the palms flat and even with each other. A clasp is when you do so with the palms curved and one hand at a 90 degree angle with the other so that they sort of fit together, almost like you're shaking hands with

To do the punch up, rest one fist on your hip and point the other one upward.

yourself. A clasp makes a slightly louder, richer sound when compared to a clap. A foot stomp can be particularly effective on a gym floor.

Beyond hand claps, clasps, and stomps, squads often use basic cheerleading moves to add emphasis and excitement to chants. These moves can be broken down into three broad categories: hand positions, arm motions, and leg positions. Moves from each category are often combined and strung together to create new moves. This is just a look at the basics to get you started.

HAND POSITIONS

Blade. To form a blade, open your hand flat and make sure that all of your fingers are pressed together. It's very much like the kind of position you would hold your hand in while diving into a pool. Make sure your thumb is tucked in tight against your hand, too. Don't hyperextend your fingers, though, or else your hand will lose its flatness and start to look like it's curved.

Bucket. To form a bucket, face your palm to the ground, then make a fist. Think of carrying a bucket of water, and you'll get the idea.

Candlestick. A candlestick is very much like a bucket, only you turn your fists so that the imaginary candle you might be holding is pointing up in the air. Your thumb should be over by your index and middle fingers, not covering the "swirl" created by your index finger.

Dagger. A dagger is another fist position, except in this case you're turning your hand so that it seems as if you're stabbing the air with a dagger.

In the arm motion known as the right diagonal, the right arm points up while the left arm points down to the ground. Pom pons can be used to accentuate arm positions.

ARM MOTIONS

Diagonal. In a diagonal, you're creating a straight line with both arms, except instead of those arms being parallel to the ground, one arm is raised and one arm is lowered. Diagonals can be called left diagonals or right diagonals, depending on which arm is pointing up. A variation of the diagonal is called the broken diagonal, in which you bend one or both of your arms at the elbows to create a shorter line.

Hands on hips. This move is exactly what it sounds like. The key here, though, is to make sure that your hands are clasped into fists, and that your fists are exactly opposite each other on your hips. If one fist is higher up on your body than the other, your body will look out of proportion and lopsided.

DON'T SCREECH

When you're chanting or cheering it is important to project your voice properly.

You want to remember to yell from your chest, not your throat. At first it might feel like your voice is deeper than it should be, but that's okay. Yelling from your throat will make you loud, and it will make you heard, but it will also strain your voice and give you a sore throat. It's not the best way to be heard in the back row.

Work on yelling from your chest and your diaphragm. Your voice will be naturally louder, and the sound will carry farther.

Try this exercise: lie on your back with your hands on your stomach, and yell your chants. If you're projecting your voice properly, you'll feel your stomach and diaphragm moving. Talk to your coach, too, about other exercises and tips you can use.

As with all the muscles in your body, your voice is something you don't want to strain.

Punch up. The punch up is when you take one arm and, while making a fist with your hand, "punch" the air so that your arm is extended straight up. Your other arm should be set in a hands on hips position. There are right punch ups and left punch ups, depending on which arm is pointing into the air. A variation of the punch up is called the punch out, in which your arms are pointed straight ahead rather than straight up.

Touchdown. Think of the touchdown as a double-arm punch up. You've probably seen referees at a football game signal a touchdown. That's exactly the kind of position you want to make. Make sure your elbows are locked and your fists are daggers. A variation of the touchdown is the low touchdown, in which your arms are pointing straight down to the ground.

L. For the L position, your arms are positioned to make the letter L. One arm will point straight up, while the other arm points straight to the side. Whether the position is called a left L or a right L depends on which arm is pointing straight up in the air.

T. Like the L position, the T mimics the capital letter after which it's named. Your arms will be extended straight out to the sides. Usually the fists are in the bucket position, but they can be in the candlestick position, too. Like the broken diagonal, the broken T is a position in which the elbows are bent to create a shorter line with the arms.

High V. In the high V position, both arms are extended over your head in diagonal position. Your arms form the sides of the letter V. Variations of the high V include the low V, in which both arms are pointing down, and the

To make the high V position, you need to keep your arms stiff and your hands in fists.

broken high V and broken low V, in which the arms are bent at the elbows. In all variations of the V, it is important to keep your arms stiff, your wrists tight, and your fists in a bucket position. In the broken versions, the pinkie sides of your fists will be facing forward.

LEG MOTIONS

Feet together. Feet together is the basic starting position for most cheerleaders. You simply stand up straight.

Posture is very important, so keep your back straight and your shoulders square. Make sure that the insides of your feet are touching each other. Feet apart is a slight variation in which you take a step to the left or right so that your feet are about shoulder width apart.

Liberty hitch. In a liberty hitch, sometimes called a stag, lift one leg so that the inside of that leg's foot is even with your other leg's knee. The toe of the leg you're lifting is pointing down to the ground. A left liberty hitch or a right liberty hitch depends on which leg you're lifting. The side liberty hitch is a slight variation in which you simply turn your body to one side.

Lunge. Start by standing with your back straight, facing forward. Set your feet wide apart, then move to one side, bending one leg so that the other leg is as straight as possible. The knee of your bent leg should be directly over your ankle. Whether you are doing a left lunge or a right lunge is determined by which leg you're bending.

These fist, arm, and leg motions are just the beginning. Be creative. You may like a certain hand position with a specific arm motion, so try it with different leg motions to see what works best. You'll soon see how some moves flow smoothly into other moves—a high V into a diagonal, for example, or vice-versa. You can also practice in the mirror, create new positions, and incorporate them into your chants. Work with your friends on your squad to come up with new ideas that work with the particular chants you are using with your team.

Once you've learned the basic positions, it's time to apply them to the specific chant you're using. For example,

When one leg is bent with the foot held up near the knee of the other leg, it is called the liberty hitch position.

consider this chant:

> *Victory! Victory!*
> *That's our cry!*
> *V-I-C-T-O-R-Y!*

A high-V with the arms might be a good way to start the chant, because the bodies of the cheerleaders will almost appear to be spelling out the first letter of the word "victory." Placing hands on hips during "That's our cry" might be a good choice for the chant because the body language is very matter-of-fact, just like the words in the chant. Together, the motions and words are saying to everyone, "We're here, we're pumped up, and we're going to win!"

There are no hard and fast rules about what positions to use when. It all depends on your personal preferences and tastes.

Here are some chants you can practice. Choose one chant, and then try mixing up the hand, arm, and leg positions you use each time you do the chant. Think about what positions work best with the words in the chant. Above all, be creative and have fun.

FOOTBALL CHANTS

For when your team has just scored a first down:

First and 10!
Do it again!

For when your team has sacked the other team's quarterback, or when the other team has lost yardage on a play:

Push 'em back! Push 'em back!
Wa-a-a-a-a-a-a-y back!

For when the other team is trying to score an extra point or a field goal:

Block that point!
Yeah!
Block that point!
Now!

For when your team seems to be on the verge of scoring a touchdown:

Time to score!
Score, score!
Six points more!

BASKETBALL CHANTS

This one is good for any team working hard to maintain the lead in a game, for when the other team has the ball:

D *(said with a stomp)*
(clap)
E-F *(said with a stomp)*
(clap)
E-N *(said with a stomp)*
(clap)
S-E *(said with a stomp)*
(clap)
(stomp-clap-stomp-clap-stomp-clap-clap)
(stomp-clap-stomp-clap-stomp-pause-clap)

Here's one for any time you want your team to score:

Shoot!
(clasp)
Shoot!
(clasp)
Shoot it (clasp) for two!
S-H-double-O-T (clasp) (clasp) for two!

Here's a chant that's appropriate for when the other team is controlling the ball:

POM PONS: YES OR NO?

Pom pons may be difficult to use in a cheer, where they might need to be picked up or put down because of some physical stunt that's taking place.

In chants, however, pom pons can be a terrific addition to the look of the squad. Pom pons accentuate arm movements and add visual emphasis to the words the fans are hearing. A chant of "Go-o-o-o-o-o team!" might sound and look great, but it could look even better if each squad member is shaking pom pons in a high-V position as they chant "Go-o-o-o-o-o." The sound of the rustling pom pons can add emphasis to a chant, too, particularly in large squads.

Try your chants with and without pom pons. See what works and what doesn't work. Remember, too, that individual tastes will enter into the picture. Some people will like a chant with pom pons, others will like it without.

That's when you may need to rely on team unity—and the opinion of your coach—to cast a deciding vote.

They got it
We want it
Now take it!
Hey! Hey!

Here's one for when someone on your team steals the ball from someone on the other team:

All the way!
Down the floor!
SCORE!

These chants are just the beginning. There are probably dozens of chants that have been in use at your school for years, many of them incorporating the names of your teams and mascots. For information on how to write your own chants and cheers, see Chapter Five. There's nothing like the feeling of leading the whole crowd at a game in a chant that you wrote yourself—and seeing that crowd energized by your own words.

CHANT AND CHEER RULES

Whether you're chanting or cheering, there are seven important rules you need to keep in mind. Each is as important as the next, so remember them all the next time you attend a cheerleading practice or step onto the playing field in front of a crowd.

1. Stay positive. This means not only keeping a positive attitude where you and your squad are concerned, it also means never crossing the line and making negative chants and cheers about the other team or squad. You and your squad are at the game to cheer for your team, not against the other team. Think positive, and be positive. If your squad chants against the other team (or even against the other squad), that says more about your squad than it does about anything else.

2. Keep smiling. It's a simple thing, but sometimes it's hard to remember. Studies have shown that smiling can be as contagious as laughter. It helps keep others in a good mood. Remembering to smile helps you improve your own mood, so it is doubly important to remember when you're not quite in a smiling mood.

3. Be complimentary. If the opportunity arises at the end of the game to say something nice about the other squad, do so. You'd feel good if they said something positive about your uniforms, cheers, chants, or stunts, so put yourself in their place. Taking the initiative to say something positive does more than build the other squad's egos. It says a lot about your squad that you're willing to do that.

4. Be crisp. When you're striking your poses and doing your chants and cheers, be crisp in your movements. Remember, people are looking at you to set a standard for enthusiasm, so don't drag yourself around on the field. Stay alert, and get a good night's sleep before cheering.

5. Be heard. Cheerleaders need to be able to project their voices and be heard. A quiet cheerleading squad is like a marching band that can't be heard. Don't expect the rest of the squad to carry the cheer for you. Let your voice be heard all the way in the back row.

6. Stay focused. Keep your mind focused on being a cheerleader, and don't let little things get to you. Remember, you're part of a team. If you get upset because someone smiled at your teammate and not at you, or if seeing your brother make a face in the stands gets you rattled, it affects more than you. It affects the whole team.

7. Always try your hardest. Maybe it's just a short chant. Maybe your team is so far behind the other team that it's impossible for them to win. That's exactly the

Facts About Cheerleaders

- 83 percent of cheerleaders carry a B average or above in high school
- 62 percent of cheerleaders are involved in a second sport
- 80 percent of schools in the United States have cheerleading squads
- 98 percent of female cheerleaders were former gymnasts
- 20 percent of male cheerleaders were former gymnasts
- 97 percent of all cheerleaders are female, but 50 percent of college cheerleaders are male
- 15 percent of all cheerleaders participate in competitions

Estimated Number of Cheerleaders in the United States

Ages 6–11	1.2 million
Ages 12–17	1.6 million
Ages 18–24	0.4 million
Ages 21–34	0.2 million

Source: www.about.com

time when you need to try your hardest. It's easy for anyone to be positive and do their best on a winning team. When your team is struggling is when your best is needed the most. Maintaining a positive attitude when something negative is happening all around you says a lot about you and your character.

Cheers

Cheers are generally longer than chants and are usually performed when the ball is not in play. Because they're longer, they give you more of a chance to be creative with both the words and the choreography you use.

Here's a cheer that can be used early in a game. For the last line, use the letters of your school. For example, if your school's name is "Keith Valley Middle School" use "K-V-M-S!"

Prepare
(pause)
For a challenge

It is essential for a cheerleader to maintain a positive attitude and outlook.

Get ready
(pause)
To meet the test
We're the team to beat
(clasp) (clasp) (clasp)
K-V-M-S

Here's another one that you can customize by adding the name of your school, your team's colors, your team's nickname, and even the nickname of the opposing team. When customizing cheers, you may need to adjust some words here and there. For example, if your school's name has four syllables in it, the cheer will have a different rhythm than if your school's name has one syllable in it.

We are
(pause)
[YOUR SCHOOL NAME] [YOUR TEAM'S COLORS]
(pause)
Reaching for the stars!
(pause)
[OPPOSING TEAM'S NICKNAME]
(pause)
Stand back!
(pause)
[YOUR TEAM'S NICKNAME] will attack!

Here's one that would be used as a "welcome cheer," a cheer that introduces the squad to the crowd, and to the other squad:

Hello!

We are the squad from [YOUR SCHOOL NAME OR LETTERS]

Our spirit is

(clap-clap)

the best!

CHOREOGRAPHING A CHEER

In Chapter Two, you learned about the various hand, arm, and leg positions that make up a cheerleader's basic repertoire. It's from those basic movements that cheer-leading choreography begins.

Once you know the words of the cheer you want to perform, you need to settle on the rhythm of the cheer. Is it said very quickly? Are there hand claps mixed in that need to be considered? Are there lines in the cheer that are long and others that are short?

Once you know how the cheer will sound, figure out how it will look. Certain words in a cheer will suggest specific hand and arm positions. For example, a high V works well with the word "victory." Also, think about what movements flow well from one to the other. That will help your choreography look smoother.

To make working on the choreography easier, try breaking the cheer down into smaller chunks. Work one or two lines at a time, and start associating movements with words. Once you've done that to the whole cheer, put it all together and try it.

Make changes here and there and try new things. Work with your coach and the other cheerleaders to come up with new ideas.

Our [YOUR TEAM NAME] pride is what you'll see
as we lead our team to victory!
We'd like to tell you who we are
We are the best
(clap-clap)
by far!
(Each cheerleader does a jump and says her name)
(The whole squad comes together in a group, chanting)
H-E-double L-O!
The [SCHOOL NAME] cheerleaders say
(clap-clap)
HELLO!

Cheerleading is as much visual as verbal, so you should use lots of hand, arm, and leg motions to choreograph your cheer. You may also want to start incorporating some basic stunting into your cheerleading.

Stunts can be thought about in two broad categories. There are partner stunts, which involve two people, and mounts, which involve three or more people.

Here are three basic partner stunts to get you started.

WARNING! Before trying any stunting, be sure to have an expert coach or trainer watching, and always use spotters. Stunting can be extremely dangerous, and even a stunt that looks very simple and safe can cause injury if done improperly. Don't take any chances. Cheer safely.

The base is the bottom person in the stunt whose feet will be on the ground. The base supports the flyer, so it's important that the base be strong and able to stay still and balanced at all times.

If you smile while cheering, your good mood will be projected into the audience.

The flyer, sometimes called the "mounter," is the person who is elevated into the air. The flyer tends to be smaller and lighter than the base, and needs to have excellent body control. The flyer needs to be aware of where the body weight is at all times. The flyer should never be pushing or pulling the base off balance.

THE PONY MOUNT

(1) The base bends her knees slightly and stands with her feet shoulder width apart. Her hands should be braced

against her thighs, just above the knees. Her elbows should be locked, and her back should be flat and rigid.

(2) The flyer stands directly behind the base, places one hand on the base's lower back, and the other hand on the base's shoulder.

(3) Using her arms to support her weight as she jumps, the flyer hops into a sitting position on the base's back. The flyer's knees are bent so that her feet are tucked in behind the base and pointing to the back

(4) Once she is sitting on the base's back, the flyer raises her arms in a high V position. Both cheerleaders

CHEERING SAFETY: THE ROLE OF THE SPOTTER

Every cheerleader wants to do stunts, and once some basic stunts are learned, every cheerleader wants to learn more advanced stunts.

Whenever you are stunting, you need to use spotters. The importance of spotters can't be emphasized enough. Their use is absolutely necessary.

It is a spotter's main responsibility to make sure that in the event of an accident, the flyer's head does not hit the ground. Beyond this responsibility, the spotter needs to know every aspect of the cheering routine. When the spotter knows the routine, she knows where the dangerous points in the routine are, and she can redouble her efforts to help insure the safety of everyone on the squad. Back spotters have particular responsibilities, too. They are the spotters who are the primary catchers of the flyers, so back spotters need to be strong, confident, and able to handle fast-moving weight.

should have their heads up, facing forward, maintaining eye contact with the crowd.

(5) To dismount, the flyer hops down as the base stands up straight. Both cheerleaders return to the hands on hips position.

THE SIDE STAND

(1) The base stands in a right lunge position, while the flyer stands behind the base's right leg and places her left foot on the base's right thigh.

(2) The flyer steps up onto the base's thigh with both feet and assumes the T position, remembering to keep her feet together. The base wraps her right arm behind the flyer's knees and rests her hand just above the flyer's right knee to provide extra support.

(3) To dismount, the flyer steps back or forward as the base remains still and uses her right arm to help guide the flyer back to the ground.

THE SHOULDER STAND

(1) The base stands in a right lunge position in front of the flyer and, extending her arms above her head, reaches out and back with her arms to join hands with the flyer.

(2) The flyer steps onto the base's right thigh with her right foot, pushes off the ground, locks the knee of her right leg, and places her left foot on the base's left shoulder.

(3) As the base provides support with her arms, the flyer presses down on her left foot and brings her right foot up onto the base's right shoulder.

A flyer does a high V while standing atop the shoulders of two bases. To come down from the shoulder stand, the flyer steps forward off the shoulders with her knees bent. The bases catch the flyer at the waist as she comes down, softening her landing.

(4) The base releases the flyer's hands one hand at a time, and places her hands behind the flyer's calves to provide extra balance and support. As the base straightens her knees, the flyer stands up straight and assumes a high V or hands on hips position.

(5) To dismount, the flyer steps forward, off the base's shoulders. The base helps the flyer to the ground by

catching the flyer at the waist with both hands. The flyer should remember to keep her knees bent and flexible as she hits the ground to minimize the impact of the dismount.

Now that you have some basic stunts to add to the hand, arm, and leg movements you learned in the last chapter, work with a coach and a spotter to practice them with your school's cheers. If you want some new cheers to work on, too, here are a few more you can try.

Watch out!
(pause)
We're back!
(pause)
We're better than before!
(pause)
So sit back and take a seat—
watch what's in store
(pause)
[YOUR TEAM'S COLORS]
Our colors
(pause)
shine through!
So get up on your feet—
(pause)
you know what to do!
YELL!
[YOUR TEAM'S COLORS]
(pause)
[YOUR TEAM'S COLORS]

In well-choreographed cheers, there are smooth transitions between the different movements.

We don't need no music!
We don't need no band!
All we need are [YOUR TEAM'S NAME] fans
Rockin' in the stands!
It goes:
(stomp-clap-stomp-stomp-clap) (three times)
Rock those stands!
(stomp-clap-stomp-stomp-clap) (three times)

One more time!
(stomp-clap-stomp-stomp-clap)
Hold up! Wait a minute!
Let me put some [YOUR TEAM NAME] in it!

(stomp-clap-stomp-stomp-clap) (three times)
Rock those stands!

Mirror, mirror, on the wall
Who's the best team of them all?
[YOUR TEAM NAME]
(stomp-stomp-stomp-stomp)
[YOUR TEAM NAME]
(stomp-stomp-stomp-stomp)
Mirror, mirror, in the stands
Who's the best team in the land?
[YOUR TEAM NAME]
(stomp-stomp-stomp-stomp)
[YOUR TEAM NAME]
(stomp-stomp stomp-stomp)
Mirror, mirror, just for fun
Tell us who is number one
[YOUR TEAM NAME]
(stomp-stomp-stomp-stomp)
[YOUR TEAM NAME]
(stomp-stomp-stomp-stomp)

Jumps

As a cheerleader, your job is to create and maintain excitement and energy. One of the best ways to do that is through the use of jumps. Well-executed jumps are eye-catching, and when a squad is able to jump in unison, it looks terrific to the crowd.

Jumps are great additions to cheers and chants. They work very well during player introductions, and are particularly appropriate after very exciting plays on the field.

Jumps should never be used when something bad happens to the other team, like a player being injured. Always remember that you're cheering for your team, not against the other team.

Flexibility is the key to the toe touch, one of the hardest jumps a cheerleader can do.

Practicing kicks can help improve your flexibility, which will make your jumps more spectacular.

Jumps have three parts: the approach, the jump itself, and the landing. Choose arm motions for the jump that work together with the jump to give you as much height as possible. The real height of the jump will come from your legs, as well as the way you swing your arms during the approach.

Before you start working on actual jumps, practice your approach to the jump. The approach gets you into the air, and gives your body the energy and momentum to get as high off the ground as possible.

Work on your approach by first standing on your toes with your arms in the high V. Keep your shoulders, head, and chest as high as you can. Next, bend your knees and bring your arms down quickly in front of you. Focus your body weight on the balls of your feet. Finally, jump straight up as hard as you can, swinging your arms up so that they're both pointing straight up in the air. The combination of jumping with your legs and swinging your arms is what will give you the height you're looking for. The better you're able to synchronize your arm and leg movements, the more height you'll achieve and the better your jump will be.

As you practice your landings, remember to keep your knees slightly bent, flexible, and loose. Land so that your feet don't hit the ground flat-footed, which invites foot injuries. Try to land on the balls of your feet, rolling from toe to heel as you land. Keep your legs slightly bent and flexible, so that they absorb the impact of the landing.

As you work on your approaches, landings, and jumps, try standing in front of a mirror and watching yourself jump so that you can figure out exactly where you want your arms and legs to be.

THE TUCK

There are many popular jumps. The tuck is a great first jump to try. It's simple, so you can concentrate on jump elements like getting good height, keeping your body straight, and landing properly and smoothly. Make fists with your hands. Jump straight in the air. When you do so, keep your feet together, bring your knees up toward your chest, and raise your arms in a high V. Work on keeping your back straight, your thighs parallel to the ground, and your toes pointed straight down.

THE SPREAD EAGLE

Jump straight in the air and spread your legs out to the sides while holding your arms in the high V position.

CHEERLEADING CAMPS

Cheerleading squads serious about performing their very best in competitions often attend a cheerleading camp to learn new routines and brush up on their overall skills. There are many kinds of cheerleading camps: sleepaway camps, day camps, summer camps, and year-round camps. Camps may be operated by small companies or by the major organizations in cheerleading such as the National Cheerleaders Association, the Universal Cheerleaders Association, and Cheerleaders of America.

What sort of experience can you expect at a cheer camp? The curriculum will vary from camp to camp but will likely include jumps, stunts, chants and cheers, pyramids, dances, routines, safety techniques, cradles, and different levels of tumbling. Some camps last one or two days, while others can last up to a week or more. The cost involved depends on the program and the length of the camp. Sometimes squads can get discounts if the group is large enough. Camps often provide special programs for coaches as well.

Point your toes and keep your legs straight. Make daggers with your hands. Like the tuck, this is a simple jump, but you should practice it a lot so you can get the feel of how to position your arms and legs properly while doing any kind of a jump. When practicing the spread eagle, try working in front of a mirror and positioning your arms and legs so that the effect is like a giant capital X.

THE DOUBLE HOOK

Sometimes referred to as a pinwheel or an abstract, the double hook is similar to a hurdler, except that both legs are bent at the knees, one in front of your body and one behind your body. Keep your back straight, make fists with your hands, and maintain your arms in a high V position.

THE HERKIE

This jump is named after Lawrence Herkimer, who started the first cheerleading company and ran the first cheerleading camp in the 1940s. It's also commonly called the side hurdler. When performing the Herkie, you kick one leg out straight to the side so that it's parallel with the ground, and you bend your other leg so that the knee is pointing to the ground. Sometimes, the Herkie is performed with the knee of the bent leg facing to the front rather than down to the ground.

THE HURDLER

The hurdler is a jump in which one leg is extended straight out in front of you and the other leg is bent at the

When working on your jumps, remember that most judges would rather see great form and less height than bad form with height.

knee and pulled up behind you. The effect looks like a runner jumping over a hurdle, hence the name. Keep your back straight, hold your arms in a high V, and remember to point your feet so that the sole of your back foot is parallel to the floor, and the toe of your front foot is pointing straight down to the floor.

THE TOE TOUCH

There's no question that this is one of the most popular jumps that cheerleaders do. It's also one of the most difficult to master. When you jump, you'll be stretching your arms straight out to your sides, and doing the same with your legs. Keep your hands open, palms flat and facing the ground. Keep your arms parallel with the ground, and bring your legs up so that you're almost touching your toes. Bringing your legs up is an important point to remember. You can achieve the same position by bringing your body down, but the overall jump won't be as high. Remember to keep your head, chest, and shoulders high, point your toes, and keep your knees and sneaker laces facing up.

WARM UP FOR JUMPS BY STRETCHING

As with any physical activity, make sure your body is ready before you begin. With jumps, that means stretching so you don't get injured while jumping. Here are a few ways to warm up before practicing your jumps.

- Practice kicking as high as you can, first with one leg, then with the other. Keep your legs and back straight as you do so. Do sets of 10 with each leg.

- Sit on the floor in a butterfly position, with your legs bent, the bottoms of your feet touching each other, and your back straight. Pull your feet in as close to your body as you can. Press down on your knees with your elbows for a count of 10.

- Standing up with your back straight, bend one leg behind you and grab your ankle. Hold the position for 30 seconds. Repeat with the other leg.

- Stand with your feet apart, wider than your shoulders. Bend at the waist slowly and reach for one of your ankles with both hands. Move your body to the middle so that one hand is on each ankle. Move your body to the other side so that both hands are reaching for the other ankle. Hold each position for about 30 seconds.

Work with your coach to develop a warm-up routine that loosens your muscles before every practice. Be sure to follow the warm-up routine at home, too.

THE DOUBLE-9

The double-9 is an interesting jump because your body creates exactly what the name of the jump is called. To do a double-9, bend at the waist and extend your left arm and left leg straight forward. Make fists with your hands. Bend your right arm at the elbow and bring your right hand to your left biceps. Bend your right leg at the knee and bring your right foot to your left thigh, just above

MAXIMIZE YOUR JUMP HEIGHT

Work with your coach to identify exercises to strengthen your legs so that you can maximize your jump height. Here's one good way you can work on jumping higher.

Start by standing straight with both feet together, then take a big step into a lunge position. Be sure to keep your back leg straight and your front knee over your front foot. With the weight of your body on your front leg, bring your back leg forward and return to a standing position. Repeat in sets of 10 with each leg.

There are many similar exercises you can do to build the kind of strength in your legs that will help maximize your jump height. Try doing crunches, too, to build up the muscles in your abdomen. When you jump, you'll be tightening your abdominals as you pull your body up into the air. As always, work with your coach to find the right exercises for you.

The repetitive practicing may seem boring, but stick with it. If you really want to maximize your abilities, this is the kind of training you'll need to do regularly. Hang in there, and before long, you'll be seeing the results.

the knee. Your arm position should mirror your leg position. The effect for the person watching the jump is that your arms are forming a "9" and your legs are forming a "9" too.

When practicing your jumps, remember to keep safety first. Always work with a coach and practice with a spotter.

Creating Your Own Chants and Cheers

You've made the squad, you're looking ahead to a new season, but you don't want to use all of the same chants and cheers your squad used last year.

Do what many squads do: write your own. There are a lot of ways to get started writing your own chants and cheers. Here are a few.

PLAYING WITH YOUR TEAM NAME

Try playing with your team name. Every team has a name, and every team name suggests its own ideas. Is your team called the Devils? Then start thinking in terms of fire, heat, and flame:

Catchy chants and cheers can get spectators on their feet and cheering, helping to increase school spirit at pep rallies and games.

We're hot
As flame
We're gonna win this game!

Is your team called the Wildcats? Then start thinking about different types of cats like tigers and lions, and about what makes them ferocious. Tigers have sharp claws. They pounce. They growl.

Wildcats are here
What do you say?
This team is going all the way!
Our claws are sharp
It's clear to see
We're on the prowl for victory!

PLAY WITH YOUR TEAM COLORS

Every school has its colors, and school colors are always a great source of pride. Think of words that rhyme with your school colors. You're out of luck if one of your school colors is orange, but you've hit the jackpot if one of them is white.

Orange, black, and white
We're here and ready to fight!

When you're writing a cheer, it's hard to go wrong if you're able to work the word "fight" into the idea. You're also in luck if one of your colors is blue, another word that rhymes pretty easily.

Come on, red and blue!
You know what we're gonna do!
We're gonna win, win, win!

Come on, red and blue!
Yeah, we're talking to you!
Let's win, win, win!

Let's go, blue!
Shoot for two!

Other school colors that work well in cheers are green (rhymes with "mean" or "fighting machine" or "toughest team you've ever seen"), black (rhymes with phrases like "we don't turn back" or "we're right on track"), and gold (rhymes with "you've been told" or "we are bold" or "never gets old").

PLAY WITH YOUR SCHOOL'S NAME

You can also get inspiration from the name of your school. That could mean using the actual name of the school, or the school initials in the cheer. Let's say, for example, you attend Keith Valley Middle School. You could start off a cheer like this:

Keith Valley fans
in the stands . . .

Or you could use the school's initials and start off a cheer like this:

K-V is here!
Stand up and cheer!

As you're working on writing your own cheers, here are a few things to keep in mind.

Remember to keep it simple. The simplest cheers and chants are the ones that get remembered the most. They're also the ones that the crowd is most likely to cheer along with, too. Your chants and cheers will also be catchier if you play around with fun rhymes. Try to write cheers with the crowd in mind. To encourage audience participation, use call and response cheers, and claps and stomps.

As you develop a cheer, try to hear what the cheer might sound like when performed by your squad. Remember that rhythm counts, too. Your chant and cheer vocabulary isn't just limited to words. You can use clap, clasp, and stomp sounds to add emphasis to your words. When used properly, these sounds can not only make a chant or cheer catchier to the ear, they can help involve the fans.

You can rewrite cheers to fit your own school situation. You can mix and match, too, taking a bit of one cheer, adding it to a piece of another cheer, and finishing off with a piece of a third cheer.

The following chants and cheers should give you plenty of ideas to get you started writing your own material.

Hey, all you [SCHOOL OR TEAM NAME] fans!
Stand up now and clap your hands!

School names, colors, mascots, and team names can all inspire new cheers.

(clap-clap-clap-clap-clap-clap-clap)
Hey, all you [SCHOOL OR TEAM NAME] fans!
Stand up now and stomp your feet!
(stomp-stomp-stomp-stomp-stomp-stomp-stomp)
Clap your hands!
(clap-clap-clap)
Stomp your feet!
(stomp-stomp-stomp)
We're a team that can't be beat!

V-I-C-T-O-R-Y
Let the freshman battle cry!
V-I-C-T-O-R-Y
Let the sophomore battle cry!
V-I-C-T-O-R-Y
Let the junior battle cry!
V-I-C-T-O-R-Y
Let the senior battle cry!
V-I-C-T-O-R-Y
Let the [NAME OF TEAM] battle cry!
Win, [NAME OF TEAM], win!

Who are you yelling for?
[NAME OF SCHOOL] [NAME OF TEAM]
Stand up and yell once more!
[NAME OF SCHOOL] [NAME OF TEAM]
Louder now, let's hear it for
[NAME OF SCHOOL] [NAME OF TEAM]
[NAME OF TEAM] fans know what to do
Pull together for you know who
Yell "Let's go team!"
(Let's go team!)
Let's go team!
(Let's go team!)

Hey, fans, stand up!
It's time to cheer
We're back on top
Again this year!
So come on, fans

Let's yell for the best!

Go, [NAME OF TEAM], go!

Hey, [NAME OF OPPOSING TEAM],

it's our time to say

Our challenge may be tough

But we wish you luck today

Our spirits go to prove

That we're ready to fight

Our team has got the power, ability, and might

So, [NAME OF OPPOSING TEAM],

it's our time to go

Our team is tough, we wish you luck

Hello!

We've got a team

That can't be beat

We never say

The word defeat

We can't be beat

Won't take defeat

We can't be beat

Won't take defeat

You know we have the spirit

You know we have the might

You know we have just what it takes

To win the game tonight!

CHANTS

Intimidate!

(clap-clap-clap)

Don't hesitate!
(clap-clap-clap)
Catch that spirit!
Come on, let's hear it!
Go [NAME OF TEAM], GO!

We're the [TEAM NAME]
Couldn't be prouder
If you can't hear us
We'll yell a little louder
(repeat, louder each time)

F-I-G-H-T
Battle on to victory!

Defense!
Do it all!
Steal that ball!

Go! fight!
Dynamite!
Push 'em back!
Hit 'em hard!
Make 'em fight for every yard!

Move it [TEAM NAME]
Move it down the field!

We're gonna split the V
Dot the I

Rock that C-T-O-R-Y
Raise your arms!
Stomp your feet!
Clap your hands
We can't be beat!
Defense
Get hot!
Hit 'em with your best shot!

We are proud of you
Yeah!
We are proud of you!

Don't be afraid to try new cheers. Above all, have fun. After all, that's what cheerleading is all about.

Glossary

back spotter – A spotter who is the primary catcher of a flyer.

base – The bottom person in a stunt who remains in contact with the floor. The base supports the mounter in a stunt.

blade – A hand position in which the hand is opened flat and all the fingers are pressed together.

bucket – A hand position in which the fingers form a fist that faces the ground, as if the person were carrying a bucket of water.

candlestick – A hand position in which the fingers form a fist that's turned to the side as if the hand were holding a candlestick.

chant – A short, repetitive yell performed continually throughout a game, or a short routine with words sometimes involving the crowd.

cheer – A longer, more spirited yell that is performed only during official breaks in a game. A cheer may utilize a variety of motions and stunts.

dagger – A hand position in which the fingers form a fist and the fist is held as if the person were stabbing the air with an imaginary dagger.

diagonal – An arm position in which both arms are extended, but one arm is raised and the other lowered, with the effect being that both arms create a straight line that's diagonal to the body.

dismount – The act of safely returning to a floor position following a stunt.

double hook – A type of jump in which both legs are bent at the knees. The double hook is also known as a pinwheel or abstract.

flyer – The person who is elevated into the air by bases to perform a mount. Sometimes called a "mounter."

Herkie – Also called the side hurdler, this is a type of jump in which one leg is straight and the other leg is bent. Named after Lawrence Herkimer, who started the first cheerleading company.

hurdler – A type of jump in which one leg is extended straight forward and the other leg is bent to the side.

jump – A spring into the air in which both feet leave the ground.

liberty hitch – A leg movement in which one leg is lifted so that the inside of that leg's foot is even with the other leg's knee; also called a stag.

lunge – A leg movement in which the feet are set wide apart, then the person moves in one direction, bending one leg so that the other leg is as straight as possible. The knee of the bent leg should be directly over that leg's ankle.

mid-base – A base who is not in contact with the cheering surface.

mount – Often used interchangeably with "stunt," a mount is any skill in which one or more persons are supported in the air.

pony mount – A partner stunt in which the flyer sits on the base's back.

punch up – An arm motion in which one arm "punches" the air so that the arm finishes extended straight up.

pyramid – A stunt involving one or more flyers supported by one or more bases and linked together.

shoulder stand – A partner stunt in which the flyer stands atop the base's shoulders.

side stand – A partner stunt in which the flyer stands atop the base, who is performing a lunge.

split – A position in which the legs are spread apart in alignment or sideways one in front of the other.

spotter – A person who is in direct contact with the floor and may help control the building of, or dismounting from, a mount.

spread eagle – A type of jump in which the arms and legs are spread out to form a giant letter X.

stunt – Any maneuver that includes tumbling, mounting, a pyramid, or a toss.

touchdown – An arm motion in which both arms are pointing straight up, in the manner of a referee signaling a touchdown.

transition – A choreographed maneuver that enables a team to move from one highlighted stunt to the next.

tuck – A type of jump during which the knees are brought up and held tightly to the chest.

tumbling – Gymnastic skills used in cheerleading.

Internet Resources

http://cheerleading.about.com/index.htm
An About.com directory of hundreds of Web sites, categorized by subject matters like Cheerleading 101, Cheers and Chants, and Fundraising.

http://www.americancheerleader.com
The official Web site of *American Cheerleader*.

http://www.cheerhome.com
CheerHome.com features news, message boards, articles, and information on cheerleading camps, competitions, and college programs.

http://www.cheerleading.net
Cheerleading.net offers links to hundreds of Web sites for cheerleaders and coaches at all levels.

http://www.cheerleading.org.uk
The Web site of the British Cheerleading Association has information about championships, camps, and clinics in the United Kingdom.

http://www.nationalspirit.com/home.asp
The National Spirit Group is the parent company of the National Cheerleaders Association (NCA), the group begun in 1948 by Lawrence Herkimer.

http://www.varsity.com
Varsity.com offers information on cheerleading and dance. The Universal Cheerleaders Association (UCA), a leader in cheerleading safety and stunt innovation, is also part of Varsity.com. The UCA is one of the largest cheerleading camp providers and competition sponsors in the world.

Further Reading

Chappell, Linda Rae. *Coaching Cheerleading Successfully.* Champaign, Illinois: Human Kinetics, 1997.

French, Stephanie Breaux. *The Cheerleading Book.* Chicago, Illinois: Contemporary Books, 1995.

Kuch, K.D. *The Cheerleaders Almanac.* New York: Random House, 1996.

McElroy, James T. *We've Got Spirit: The Life and Times of America's Greatest Cheerleading Team.* New York: Berkley Books, 1999.

Neil, Randy, and Elaine Hart. *The Official Cheerleader's Handbook.* New York: Fireside Books, 1986.

Index

PICTURE CREDITS
Front cover: Tim Jackson Photography
Back cover: United Spirit Association (USA)

Tim Jackson Photography: 2, 6, 11, 12, 15, 18, 20, 28, 33, 36, 38, 40, 50, 55; Courtesy of the United Spirit Association (USA): 42, 46.

CRAIG PETERS has been writing about various aspects of sports and popular culture for more than two decades. His daughter, Alexandra, began her dance and cheerleading training when she was two years old. By the age of 13, Alexandra had competed on several school and recreation teams and been named captain of her middle school cheerleading squad. Craig has long ago given up the idea that this might be a passing fad for his daughter.